# 50 Premium Drink Recipes

By: Kelly Johnson

# Table of Contents

- Spiced Apple Cider
- Elderflower Gin Fizz
- Smoky Mezcal Margarita
- Salted Caramel Martini
- Hibiscus Iced Tea
- Lemon Basil Mojito
- Lavender Lemonade
- Matcha Latte
- Raspberry Mule
- Bourbon Peach Smash
- Coconut Water Cooler
- Pineapple Ginger Punch
- French 75
- Pomegranate Champagne Cocktail
- Watermelon Frosé
- Blackberry Mojito
- Cucumber Mint Gimlet
- Ginger Lime Cooler
- Apple Cinnamon Whiskey Sour
- Blood Orange Sangria
- Hot Buttered Rum
- Spicy Pineapple Margarita
- Rose Lemonade
- Coconut Mojito
- Chocolate Martini
- Champagne Mule
- Saffron Lemon Iced Tea
- Chai Spiced Whiskey Sour
- Strawberry Gin Fizz
- Blueberry Lemon Smash
- Sweet Peach Iced Tea
- Raspberry Bellini
- Cinnamon Roll Old Fashioned
- Mango Mojito
- Apricot Bourbon Smash

- Grapefruit and Sage Spritz
- Lemon Rosemary Gin & Tonic
- Cantaloupe Cooler
- Tiramisu Martini
- Spiced Pumpkin Latte
- Tropical Mai Tai
- Poppyseed Lemonade
- Green Tea Mojito
- Black Currant Daiquiri
- Peach Tea Fizz
- Watermelon Sangria
- Maple Bourbon Latte
- Lavender Peach Fizz
- Cranberry Mojito
- Mango Coconut Smoothie

## Spiced Apple Cider

**Ingredients:**

- 4 cups apple cider
- 1 cinnamon stick
- 2-3 whole cloves
- 1-2 star anise
- 1 orange, sliced
- 1 tablespoon brown sugar (optional)

**Instructions:**

1. In a pot, combine apple cider, cinnamon stick, cloves, star anise, and orange slices.
2. Heat over medium heat, stirring occasionally.
3. Let simmer for 10-15 minutes to allow the spices to infuse.
4. Strain and serve hot, optionally adding brown sugar for extra sweetness.

## Elderflower Gin Fizz

**Ingredients:**

- 2 oz gin
- 1 oz elderflower liqueur (such as St-Germain)
- 1/2 oz fresh lemon juice
- 1 egg white (optional for foam)
- Club soda
- Ice
- Lemon twist for garnish

**Instructions:**

1. In a cocktail shaker, combine gin, elderflower liqueur, lemon juice, and egg white (if using).
2. Shake well for 10-15 seconds without ice (dry shake) to create foam.
3. Add ice and shake again for 10-15 seconds.
4. Strain into a glass and top with club soda.
5. Garnish with a lemon twist.

## Smoky Mezcal Margarita

**Ingredients:**

- 2 oz mezcal
- 1 oz lime juice
- 1/2 oz orange liqueur (such as Cointreau)
- 1/4 oz agave syrup (optional)
- Salt for rim
- Lime wheel for garnish

**Instructions:**

1. Rim a glass with lime and salt.
2. In a cocktail shaker, combine mezcal, lime juice, orange liqueur, and agave syrup (if using).
3. Add ice and shake well.
4. Strain into the prepared glass.
5. Garnish with a lime wheel.

## Salted Caramel Martini

**Ingredients:**

- 2 oz vodka
- 1 oz salted caramel liqueur
- 1 oz cream or milk
- Caramel sauce for garnish
- Sea salt for rimming

**Instructions:**

1. Rim a martini glass with caramel sauce and sea salt.
2. In a shaker, combine vodka, salted caramel liqueur, and cream.
3. Add ice and shake well.
4. Strain into the prepared glass.
5. Garnish with a drizzle of caramel sauce and a pinch of sea salt.

**Hibiscus Iced Tea**

**Ingredients:**

- 1/4 cup dried hibiscus flowers
- 4 cups water
- 2 tablespoons honey or sugar (optional)
- Ice
- Fresh mint or lime wedges for garnish

**Instructions:**

1. Bring water to a boil and pour over dried hibiscus flowers in a heatproof container.
2. Let steep for about 10-15 minutes, then strain.
3. Sweeten with honey or sugar if desired, and let cool to room temperature.
4. Serve over ice, garnished with fresh mint or lime wedges.

**Lemon Basil Mojito**

**Ingredients:**

- 2 oz white rum
- 1 oz fresh lemon juice
- 1 tablespoon honey or simple syrup
- 8-10 fresh basil leaves
- Club soda
- Ice
- Lemon wheel and basil sprig for garnish

**Instructions:**

1. Muddle the basil leaves with lemon juice and honey (or simple syrup) in a glass.
2. Add rum and fill the glass with ice.
3. Top with club soda and stir gently.
4. Garnish with a lemon wheel and basil sprig.

## Lavender Lemonade

**Ingredients:**

- 1/2 cup fresh lemon juice
- 1/4 cup honey or sugar
- 1 teaspoon dried lavender flowers
- 4 cups water
- Ice
- Lemon slices and lavender sprigs for garnish

**Instructions:**

1. In a small saucepan, combine 1 cup of water and lavender flowers.
2. Bring to a simmer, then remove from heat and let steep for 10 minutes.
3. Strain the lavender syrup into a pitcher and add lemon juice, honey (or sugar), and the remaining water.
4. Stir until dissolved, then refrigerate to chill.
5. Serve over ice, garnished with lemon slices and lavender sprigs.

## Matcha Latte

**Ingredients:**

- 1 teaspoon matcha powder
- 1 tablespoon hot water
- 1 cup milk (dairy or non-dairy)
- 1 teaspoon honey or sweetener (optional)

**Instructions:**

1. Whisk the matcha powder and hot water in a bowl until smooth and frothy.
2. Heat the milk in a saucepan until hot (but not boiling).
3. Pour the matcha mixture into a cup and slowly add the heated milk, stirring gently.
4. Sweeten with honey or your preferred sweetener.
5. Serve hot, optionally garnished with a sprinkle of matcha powder.

**Raspberry Mule**

**Ingredients:**

- 2 oz vodka
- 1 oz lime juice
- 1 oz raspberry purée
- 3 oz ginger beer
- Fresh raspberries and mint for garnish
- Ice

**Instructions:**

1. In a copper mug or glass, combine vodka, lime juice, and raspberry purée.
2. Add ice and top with ginger beer.
3. Stir gently to combine.
4. Garnish with fresh raspberries and mint leaves.

**Bourbon Peach Smash**

**Ingredients:**

- 2 oz bourbon
- 1 oz peach nectar or purée
- 1/2 oz fresh lemon juice
- 1/2 oz simple syrup
- 4-5 fresh mint leaves
- Ice
- Peach slice for garnish

**Instructions:**

1. Muddle mint leaves in a shaker with lemon juice and simple syrup.
2. Add bourbon, peach nectar, and ice.
3. Shake well and strain into a glass filled with ice.
4. Garnish with a peach slice and a sprig of mint.

## Coconut Water Cooler

**Ingredients:**

- 2 oz coconut water
- 1 oz lime juice
- 1 oz agave syrup (or simple syrup)
- 3 oz soda water
- Ice
- Lime wedges and mint sprig for garnish

**Instructions:**

1. In a shaker, combine coconut water, lime juice, and agave syrup.
2. Shake well with ice and strain into a glass filled with ice.
3. Top with soda water and stir gently.
4. Garnish with lime wedges and a mint sprig.

## Pineapple Ginger Punch

**Ingredients:**

- 2 cups pineapple juice
- 1/2 cup ginger ale
- 1/4 cup fresh lime juice
- 1 tablespoon honey or sugar (optional)
- Ice
- Pineapple wedges and mint for garnish

**Instructions:**

1. In a large pitcher, combine pineapple juice, ginger ale, and lime juice.
2. Stir in honey or sugar if desired to sweeten.
3. Fill glasses with ice and pour the punch over.
4. Garnish with pineapple wedges and fresh mint.

## French 75

**Ingredients:**

- 1 oz gin
- 1/2 oz fresh lemon juice
- 1/2 oz simple syrup
- 3 oz champagne or sparkling wine
- Lemon twist for garnish

**Instructions:**

1. In a cocktail shaker, combine gin, lemon juice, and simple syrup with ice.
2. Shake well and strain into a champagne flute.
3. Top with champagne or sparkling wine.
4. Garnish with a lemon twist.

## Pomegranate Champagne Cocktail

**Ingredients:**

- 1 oz pomegranate juice
- 1/2 oz orange liqueur (such as Cointreau)
- 3 oz champagne or sparkling wine
- Pomegranate seeds for garnish

**Instructions:**

1. Pour pomegranate juice and orange liqueur into a champagne flute.
2. Top with champagne or sparkling wine.
3. Stir gently and garnish with pomegranate seeds.

## Watermelon Frosé

**Ingredients:**

- 2 cups frozen watermelon cubes
- 1 1/2 cups rosé wine
- 1 oz lime juice
- 1 tablespoon honey or simple syrup
- Mint leaves for garnish

**Instructions:**

1. In a blender, combine frozen watermelon, rosé wine, lime juice, and honey.
2. Blend until smooth and frosty.
3. Pour into glasses and garnish with mint leaves.

**Blackberry Mojito**

**Ingredients:**

- 2 oz white rum
- 1/2 oz lime juice
- 1/2 oz simple syrup
- 8-10 fresh blackberries
- 6-8 fresh mint leaves
- Soda water
- Ice
- Blackberry and mint for garnish

**Instructions:**

1. Muddle blackberries and mint leaves in a glass.
2. Add rum, lime juice, and simple syrup.
3. Fill the glass with ice and top with soda water.
4. Stir gently and garnish with a blackberry and mint sprig.

## Cucumber Mint Gimlet

**Ingredients:**

- 2 oz gin
- 1 oz fresh lime juice
- 1/2 oz simple syrup
- 4-5 cucumber slices
- 6-8 fresh mint leaves
- Ice
- Cucumber slice and mint sprig for garnish

**Instructions:**

1. Muddle cucumber slices and mint leaves in a cocktail shaker.
2. Add gin, lime juice, and simple syrup with ice.
3. Shake well and strain into a glass filled with ice.
4. Garnish with a cucumber slice and a mint sprig.

**Ginger Lime Cooler**

**Ingredients:**

- 2 oz ginger beer
- 1 oz lime juice
- 1/2 oz honey or simple syrup
- 2 oz club soda
- Ice
- Lime wedge and mint sprig for garnish

**Instructions:**

1. In a glass, combine lime juice and honey or simple syrup.
2. Add ice and ginger beer, then top with club soda.
3. Stir gently to combine.
4. Garnish with a lime wedge and a sprig of mint.

## Apple Cinnamon Whiskey Sour

**Ingredients:**

- 2 oz bourbon or whiskey
- 1 oz apple cider
- 1/2 oz lemon juice
- 1/4 oz cinnamon syrup (or regular simple syrup with a pinch of cinnamon)
- Ice
- Apple slice and cinnamon stick for garnish

**Instructions:**

1. In a cocktail shaker, combine bourbon, apple cider, lemon juice, and cinnamon syrup with ice.
2. Shake well and strain into a glass filled with ice.
3. Garnish with an apple slice and a cinnamon stick.

## Blood Orange Sangria

**Ingredients:**

- 1 bottle red wine (Cabernet Sauvignon or Merlot)
- 1/2 cup blood orange juice
- 1/4 cup brandy
- 1/4 cup simple syrup
- 1 orange, sliced
- 1 lemon, sliced
- 1 apple, sliced
- 2-3 blood oranges, sliced
- Ice

**Instructions:**

1. In a large pitcher, combine wine, blood orange juice, brandy, and simple syrup.
2. Add the sliced fruits and stir gently.
3. Refrigerate for at least 2 hours to allow the flavors to meld.
4. Serve over ice.

## Hot Buttered Rum

**Ingredients:**

- 2 oz dark rum
- 1 tablespoon unsalted butter
- 1 tablespoon brown sugar
- 1/4 teaspoon ground cinnamon
- 1/4 teaspoon ground nutmeg
- Boiling water
- Cinnamon stick and orange peel for garnish

**Instructions:**

1. In a mug, combine butter, brown sugar, cinnamon, and nutmeg.
2. Add rum and stir until the butter melts.
3. Top with boiling water and stir to combine.
4. Garnish with a cinnamon stick and orange peel.

**Spicy Pineapple Margarita**

**Ingredients:**

- 2 oz tequila
- 1 oz lime juice
- 1 oz pineapple juice
- 1/2 oz triple sec
- 2-3 slices jalapeño (seeds removed)
- Tajín seasoning or salt for rimming the glass
- Ice
- Pineapple wedge and jalapeño slice for garnish

**Instructions:**

1. Rim a glass with Tajín seasoning or salt.
2. In a shaker, combine tequila, lime juice, pineapple juice, triple sec, and jalapeño slices with ice.
3. Shake well and strain into the rimmed glass filled with ice.
4. Garnish with a pineapple wedge and jalapeño slice.

## Rose Lemonade

**Ingredients:**

- 1 oz rose syrup
- 1 oz fresh lemon juice
- 1/2 oz simple syrup
- 3 oz sparkling water or club soda
- Ice
- Lemon slice and rose petal for garnish

**Instructions:**

1. In a glass, combine rose syrup, lemon juice, and simple syrup.
2. Fill the glass with ice and top with sparkling water.
3. Stir gently and garnish with a lemon slice and a rose petal.

## Coconut Mojito

**Ingredients:**

- 2 oz rum
- 1 oz coconut cream
- 1/2 oz fresh lime juice
- 6-8 fresh mint leaves
- 1/2 oz simple syrup
- Soda water
- Ice
- Mint sprig and lime wedge for garnish

**Instructions:**

1. Muddle mint leaves with lime juice and simple syrup in a shaker.
2. Add rum, coconut cream, and ice.
3. Shake well and strain into a glass filled with ice.
4. Top with soda water and garnish with a mint sprig and lime wedge.

**Chocolate Martini**

**Ingredients:**

- 2 oz vodka
- 1 oz chocolate liqueur
- 1 oz cream or milk
- 1/2 oz simple syrup (optional)
- Chocolate shavings or cocoa powder for garnish

**Instructions:**

1. In a shaker, combine vodka, chocolate liqueur, cream, and simple syrup with ice.
2. Shake well and strain into a chilled martini glass.
3. Garnish with chocolate shavings or a sprinkle of cocoa powder.

**Champagne Mule**

**Ingredients:**

- 1 oz vodka
- 1/2 oz lime juice
- 1/2 oz simple syrup
- 3 oz champagne or sparkling wine
- Ginger beer
- Ice
- Lime wedge and mint sprig for garnish

**Instructions:**

1. In a shaker, combine vodka, lime juice, simple syrup, and ice.
2. Shake well and strain into a glass filled with ice.
3. Top with champagne and ginger beer.
4. Stir gently and garnish with a lime wedge and mint sprig.

## Saffron Lemon Iced Tea

**Ingredients:**

- 4 cups water
- 2 black tea bags
- 1/4 teaspoon saffron threads
- 1/4 cup fresh lemon juice
- 2 tablespoons honey (or to taste)
- Ice
- Lemon slices and mint sprigs for garnish

**Instructions:**

1. Bring 2 cups of water to a boil, add saffron threads, and let them steep for 5 minutes.
2. In a separate pot, brew the tea bags with the remaining 2 cups of water for about 5 minutes.
3. Combine the brewed tea and saffron water in a large pitcher, and add lemon juice and honey. Stir until the honey dissolves.
4. Let the tea chill in the refrigerator.
5. Serve over ice and garnish with lemon slices and mint sprigs.

## Chai Spiced Whiskey Sour

**Ingredients:**

- 2 oz bourbon
- 1 oz chai syrup (or 1/2 tsp chai spice mix and 1/2 oz simple syrup)
- 3/4 oz fresh lemon juice
- 1 egg white (optional, for froth)
- Ice
- Lemon twist for garnish

**Instructions:**

1. In a cocktail shaker, combine bourbon, chai syrup, lemon juice, and egg white (if using).
2. Shake vigorously without ice for 10 seconds to froth the egg white, then add ice and shake again.
3. Strain into a glass with ice.
4. Garnish with a lemon twist.

**Strawberry Gin Fizz**

**Ingredients:**

- 2 oz gin
- 1/4 cup fresh strawberries, mashed
- 1 oz lemon juice
- 1/2 oz simple syrup
- Club soda
- Ice
- Strawberry slice for garnish

**Instructions:**

1. In a cocktail shaker, muddle the strawberries with lemon juice and simple syrup.
2. Add gin and ice, then shake until well chilled.
3. Strain into a glass filled with ice and top with club soda.
4. Garnish with a strawberry slice.

## Blueberry Lemon Smash

**Ingredients:**

- 2 oz vodka
- 1/4 cup fresh blueberries
- 1 oz fresh lemon juice
- 1/2 oz simple syrup
- Club soda
- Ice
- Lemon wheel and blueberries for garnish

**Instructions:**

1. Muddle the blueberries with lemon juice and simple syrup in a shaker.
2. Add vodka and ice, then shake well.
3. Strain into a glass filled with ice and top with club soda.
4. Garnish with a lemon wheel and extra blueberries.

## Sweet Peach Iced Tea

**Ingredients:**

- 4 cups water
- 2 black tea bags
- 1/2 cup peach nectar
- 2 tablespoons honey (or to taste)
- Ice
- Peach slices and mint sprigs for garnish

**Instructions:**

1. Brew the black tea by steeping the tea bags in 4 cups of boiling water for about 5 minutes.
2. Remove the tea bags and stir in peach nectar and honey until the honey dissolves.
3. Let the tea cool and refrigerate until chilled.
4. Serve over ice and garnish with peach slices and mint sprigs.

**Raspberry Bellini**

**Ingredients:**

- 2 oz raspberry purée
- 4 oz Prosecco or sparkling wine
- 1/2 oz fresh lemon juice
- Fresh raspberries for garnish

**Instructions:**

1. In a glass, combine raspberry purée and lemon juice.
2. Top with chilled Prosecco or sparkling wine.
3. Stir gently and garnish with fresh raspberries.

**Cinnamon Roll Old Fashioned**

**Ingredients:**

- 2 oz bourbon
- 1/4 oz cinnamon syrup (or 1 cinnamon stick)
- 2 dashes Angostura bitters
- Orange peel
- Ice

**Instructions:**

1. In a mixing glass, combine bourbon, cinnamon syrup (or a cinnamon stick), and bitters.
2. Add ice and stir until chilled.
3. Strain into a glass with a large ice cube.
4. Garnish with orange peel.

## Mango Mojito

**Ingredients:**

- 2 oz rum
- 1/4 cup fresh mango chunks
- 1 oz fresh lime juice
- 6-8 mint leaves
- 1/2 oz simple syrup
- Club soda
- Ice
- Lime wedge and mint sprig for garnish

**Instructions:**

1. Muddle mango chunks, lime juice, and mint leaves in a shaker.
2. Add rum and simple syrup with ice, then shake well.
3. Strain into a glass filled with ice and top with club soda.
4. Garnish with a lime wedge and mint sprig.

**Apricot Bourbon Smash**

**Ingredients:**

- 2 oz bourbon
- 3 fresh apricots, pitted and quartered
- 1 oz fresh lemon juice
- 1/2 oz honey syrup
- Ice
- Lemon twist for garnish

**Instructions:**

1. Muddle apricot quarters with lemon juice and honey syrup in a shaker.
2. Add bourbon and ice, then shake well.
3. Strain into a glass filled with ice.
4. Garnish with a lemon twist.

## Grapefruit and Sage Spritz

**Ingredients:**

- 2 oz grapefruit juice
- 1 oz gin
- 1/2 oz elderflower liqueur
- 3-4 fresh sage leaves
- Club soda
- Ice
- Grapefruit slices and sage sprigs for garnish

**Instructions:**

1. In a shaker, muddle the fresh sage leaves with grapefruit juice.
2. Add gin and elderflower liqueur, then shake with ice.
3. Strain into a glass filled with ice and top with club soda.
4. Garnish with grapefruit slices and sage sprigs.

## Lemon Rosemary Gin & Tonic

**Ingredients:**

- 2 oz gin
- 1 oz fresh lemon juice
- 1/2 oz rosemary simple syrup (or rosemary sprig)
- Tonic water
- Ice
- Lemon wheel and rosemary sprig for garnish

**Instructions:**

1. Combine gin, lemon juice, and rosemary syrup (or a rosemary sprig) in a shaker with ice.
2. Shake and strain into a glass filled with ice.
3. Top with tonic water and stir gently.
4. Garnish with a lemon wheel and a rosemary sprig.

## Cantaloupe Cooler

**Ingredients:**

- 1 cup cantaloupe, cubed
- 2 oz vodka
- 1 oz fresh lime juice
- 1/2 oz simple syrup
- Club soda
- Ice
- Cantaloupe slices and mint sprigs for garnish

**Instructions:**

1. Muddle the cantaloupe with lime juice and simple syrup in a shaker.
2. Add vodka and ice, then shake until chilled.
3. Strain into a glass filled with ice and top with club soda.
4. Garnish with cantaloupe slices and mint sprigs.

## Tiramisu Martini

**Ingredients:**

- 2 oz vodka
- 1 oz coffee liqueur (e.g., Kahlúa)
- 1 oz mascarpone cheese
- 1 oz heavy cream
- 1/2 oz simple syrup
- Cocoa powder for garnish
- Ice

**Instructions:**

1. Combine vodka, coffee liqueur, mascarpone, cream, and simple syrup in a shaker with ice.
2. Shake vigorously until well-chilled and creamy.
3. Strain into a chilled martini glass.
4. Garnish with a dusting of cocoa powder.

## Spiced Pumpkin Latte

**Ingredients:**

- 1/2 cup brewed espresso
- 1/2 cup milk (or plant-based milk)
- 2 tbsp pumpkin purée
- 1 tbsp sugar (or to taste)
- 1/2 tsp pumpkin spice
- Whipped cream
- Ground cinnamon for garnish

**Instructions:**

1. In a saucepan, heat milk, pumpkin purée, sugar, and pumpkin spice over medium heat until warm.
2. Whisk until smooth and frothy.
3. Brew a shot of espresso and pour into a mug.
4. Add the pumpkin milk mixture to the espresso and stir.
5. Top with whipped cream and a sprinkle of ground cinnamon.

**Tropical Mai Tai**

**Ingredients:**

- 1 oz white rum
- 1 oz dark rum
- 1/2 oz orange liqueur
- 1/2 oz lime juice
- 1/2 oz orgeat syrup
- Pineapple juice
- Ice
- Lime wheel and mint sprig for garnish

**Instructions:**

1. In a shaker, combine white rum, dark rum, orange liqueur, lime juice, and orgeat syrup with ice.
2. Shake well and strain into a glass filled with crushed ice.
3. Top with a splash of pineapple juice.
4. Garnish with a lime wheel and mint sprig.

## Poppyseed Lemonade

**Ingredients:**

- 1 cup fresh lemon juice
- 1/2 cup simple syrup
- 1 tablespoon poppy seeds
- 3 cups cold water
- Ice
- Lemon slices for garnish

**Instructions:**

1. In a pitcher, combine lemon juice, simple syrup, poppy seeds, and cold water.
2. Stir until well mixed.
3. Serve over ice and garnish with lemon slices.

## Green Tea Mojito

**Ingredients:**

- 2 oz white rum
- 1 oz green tea (cooled)
- 1 oz lime juice
- 1/2 oz simple syrup
- 6-8 fresh mint leaves
- Club soda
- Ice
- Lime wedge and mint sprig for garnish

**Instructions:**

1. Muddle mint leaves and lime juice in a shaker.
2. Add rum, green tea, simple syrup, and ice, then shake.
3. Strain into a glass filled with ice and top with club soda.
4. Garnish with a lime wedge and mint sprig.

## Black Currant Daiquiri

**Ingredients:**

- 2 oz white rum
- 1 oz black currant liqueur (such as Crème de Cassis)
- 1 oz fresh lime juice
- 1/2 oz simple syrup
- Ice
- Lime wheel for garnish

**Instructions:**

1. Combine rum, black currant liqueur, lime juice, and simple syrup in a shaker with ice.
2. Shake until well-chilled.
3. Strain into a chilled glass.
4. Garnish with a lime wheel.

## Peach Tea Fizz

**Ingredients:**

- 1 oz peach vodka
- 1 oz iced tea
- 1/2 oz lemon juice
- 1/2 oz simple syrup
- Club soda
- Ice
- Peach slice for garnish

**Instructions:**

1. Combine peach vodka, iced tea, lemon juice, and simple syrup in a shaker with ice.
2. Shake and strain into a tall glass filled with ice.
3. Top with club soda.
4. Garnish with a peach slice.

## Watermelon Sangria

**Ingredients:**

- 3 cups watermelon, cubed
- 1 bottle dry white wine
- 1/2 cup brandy
- 1/4 cup orange liqueur (like Triple Sec)
- 1/4 cup simple syrup
- 1 cup soda water or club soda
- Ice
- Mint sprigs for garnish

**Instructions:**

1. In a blender, blend the watermelon until smooth.
2. In a large pitcher, combine the watermelon puree, wine, brandy, orange liqueur, and simple syrup.
3. Stir well and chill in the refrigerator for at least 2 hours.
4. Before serving, add ice and top with club soda.
5. Garnish with mint sprigs.

**Maple Bourbon Latte**

**Ingredients:**

- 1 oz bourbon
- 1/2 oz maple syrup
- 1/2 cup brewed espresso
- 1/2 cup steamed milk (or plant-based milk)
- Ground cinnamon for garnish

**Instructions:**

1. In a glass, combine bourbon and maple syrup.
2. Brew a shot of espresso and pour it over the maple mixture.
3. Add steamed milk and stir gently.
4. Garnish with a sprinkle of ground cinnamon.

## Lavender Peach Fizz

**Ingredients:**

- 1 oz peach schnapps
- 1/2 oz lavender syrup
- 1 oz fresh lemon juice
- Club soda
- Ice
- Lavender sprig for garnish

**Instructions:**

1. Combine peach schnapps, lavender syrup, and lemon juice in a shaker with ice.
2. Shake well and strain into a glass filled with ice.
3. Top with club soda.
4. Garnish with a lavender sprig.

**Cranberry Mojito**

**Ingredients:**

- 2 oz white rum
- 1/2 oz cranberry juice
- 1 oz fresh lime juice
- 1/2 oz simple syrup
- 6-8 fresh mint leaves
- Club soda
- Ice
- Lime wedge and mint sprig for garnish

**Instructions:**

1. Muddle mint leaves and lime juice in a shaker.
2. Add rum, cranberry juice, simple syrup, and ice.
3. Shake well and strain into a glass filled with ice.
4. Top with club soda and garnish with a lime wedge and mint sprig.

**Mango Coconut Smoothie**

**Ingredients:**

- 1 cup frozen mango chunks
- 1/2 cup coconut milk (or coconut water for a lighter option)
- 1/2 banana
- 1/2 tsp vanilla extract
- Ice

**Instructions:**

1. Combine mango, coconut milk, banana, vanilla extract, and ice in a blender.
2. Blend until smooth and creamy.
3. Pour into a glass and serve immediately.

www.ingramcontent.com/pod-product-compliance
Lightning Source LLC
LaVergne TN
LVHW081459060526
838201LV00056BA/2839